D1714757

GOING FAST

GOING FAST

Frederick Seidel

POEMS

FARRAR, STRAUS AND GIROUX

NEW YORK

Farrar, Straus and Giroux
19 Union Square West, New York 10003

Distributed in Canada by Douglas & McIntyre Ltd.

Printed in the United States of America

Designed by Peter A. Andersen

First edition, 1998

Library of Congress Cataloging-in-Publication Data

Seidel, Frederick, 1936–

  Going fast : poems / Frederick Seidel.—1st ed.

  p. cm.

  ISBN 0-374-16488-6 (alk. paper)

  I. Title.

  PS3569.E5G65 1998

  811'.54—dc21   97-48273

TO RICHARD POIRIER

CONTENTS

FOR A NEW PLANETARIUM

NEW YORK

LONDON

PARIS & TAHITI

FASTER

MILAN

BOLOGNA

GOING FAST

FOR A NEW PLANETARIUM

MIDNIGHT

God begins. The universe will soon.
The intensity of the baseball bat
Meets the ball. Is the fireball
When he speaks and then in the silence
The cobra head rises regally and turns to look at you.
The angel burns through the air.
The flower turns to look.

The cover of the book opens on its own.
You do not want to see what is on this page.
It looks up at you,
Only it is a mirror you are looking into.
The truth is there, and all around the truth fire
Makes a frame.
Listen. An angel. These sounds you hear are his.

A dog is barking in a field.
A car starts in the parking lot on the other side.
The ocean heaves back and forth three blocks away.
The fire in the wood stove eases
The inflamed cast-iron door
Open, steps out into the room across the freezing floor
To your perfumed bed where as it happens you kneel and pray.

PRAYER

But we are someone else. We're born that way.
The other one we are lives in a distant city.
People are walking down a street.
They pop umbrellas open when it starts to rain.
Some stand under an apartment building awning.
A doorman dashes out into the spring shower for
A taxi with its off-duty light on that hisses right past.
The daffodils are out on the avenue center strip.
The yellow cabs are yellow as the daffodils.
One exhausted driver, at the end of his ten-hour shift headed in,
Stops for the other one
We are who hides among the poor
And looks like the homeless out on the wet street corner.
Dear friend, get in.
I will take you where you're going for free.
Only a child's Crayola
Could color a taxi cab this yellow
In a distant city full of yellow flowers.

THE NIGHT SKY

At night, when she is fast asleep,
The comet, which appears not to move at all,
Crosses the sky above her bed,
But stays there looking down.

She rises from her sleeping body.
Her body stays behind asleep.
She climbs the lowered ladder.
She enters through the opened hatch.

Inside is everyone.
Everyone is there.
Someone smiling is made of silk.
Someone else was made with milk.

Her mother still alive.
Her brothers and sisters and father
And aunts and uncles and grandparents
And husband never died.

Hold the glass with both hands,
My darling, that way you won't spill.
On her little dress, her cloth yellow star
Comet travels through space.

STARS

None of the Above
Stays down here below.
My going very fast
Describes the atmosphere.
Heady.

And when I die,
We orbit way
Above the sky of
And return
From stars.

We fall from stars
In all the colors of Brazil,
Of Africa, Iran.
We stir a black hole swirl, star
Figure skaters twirling on the black, galaxies

Unspooling on the surface tension
Of the morning coffee
In the cup.
The little bubble prickles
Are a house, a dog, a car.

One day an asteroid will come,
A mountain coming from the sky,
And from a long way off at last
The truth will see
Nothing can be done and nothing can remain.

THE STARS ABOVE
THE EMPTY QUARTER

A cat has caught a mouse and is playing
At letting it go is the sun
Over the desert letting the traveler reach the oasis.
The sink vomits all over itself
Is the sand boiling down from the blond sky in a storm.
A pre-Islamic Golden Ode lists
The hundred qualities of a camel.
Suavity, power, the beauty of its eyes.
Its horn, its tires, its perfect bumpers, its perfect fenders.
The way it turns left, the way it turns right.
The great poet Labīd sings
His Song of Songs about the one he loves.
How long it can go without water and without God.
Sings the nomad life of hardship, calls it ease.
He stares at the far-off stars.
He mounts the kneeling camel at dawn.
He lowers himself and rises.
I sing above the sand under the sun.

CONTENTS UNDER PRESSURE

His space suit is his respirator breathing him
From its own limited supply of oxygen.
The hand-controlled jet nozzles squirted him away
On a space walk in short bursts that have gone haywire.
But will stop when there is no fuel seconds from now. Now.
The long tether back to the mother spaceship sticks
Straight out from his back weightlessly
In the zero gravity of space.
It has sheared off at the other end.
Absolutely nothing can be done.
The spacecraft is under orders not to try and to return and does.
He urinates and defecates
And looks out at the universe.
He is looking out at it through his helmet mask.

NEW YORK

AT GRACIE MANSION

I like motorcycles, the city, the telephone.
TV but not to watch, just to turn it on.
The women and their legs, the movies and the streets.
At dawn when it's so hot the sky is almost red.
The smell of both the rivers is the underworld exhumed.

I remember the vanished days of the great steakhouses.
Before the miniaturization in electronics.
When Robert Wagner was mayor and men ate meat.
I like air conditioning, leather booths, linen,
Heat, Milan, Thomas Jefferson.

The woman got red in the face touching her girlfriend live
On one of the cable public access shows you do yourself.
Part of the redundancy built into servo systems
That can fail was when she started to spank the girl.
I took her heat straight to my heart.

I never watch TV.
But sometimes late at night. My friend
The junior senator from Nebraska, the only
Medal of Honor winner in Congress, reads Mandelstam,
Reads Joseph Roth. What happens next?

When Wagner's first wife died of cancer,
And Bennett Cerf died of cancer,

Phyllis Cerf and Bob got married—and then Bob died of cancer.
Bobby, Jr., restored by Giuliani, dropped dead on a plane to L.A.
At the age of forty-nine.

How's that again?
Bobby died suddenly in a hotel room in San Antonio.
Bennett expired from Parkinson's.
It ought to matter what battlefield you died on.
A deputy mayor under Koch and the founder of
        Random House.

I like it when the long line of headlights on behind the
        hearse
Is stuck in backed-up traffic on the Drive.
A tug tows a barge slowly by
The closed smoked-glass windows of the limousines.
I read Olmsted. I kiss the Parks Commissioner.

I like anything worth dying for.
I like the brave. I like the Type A personality which is hot.
I like the hideous embarrassment of Nelson Rockefeller
Dying inside somebody young.
He had an attack heart.

I watch a floater in my eye cross Jimmy Walker on the wall.
I like the bead curtains of hot rain outside on the street.
I hold a "see-through on a stem," an ice-cold martini.
Take the heat in your hand. It is cold.
Take the heat. Drink.

THE PIERRE HOTEL,
NEW YORK, 1946

The bowl of a silver spoon held candlelight,
A glistening oyster of gold.
The linen between us was snowblind, blinding white.
I felt a weight too light to weigh
Which was my wings.

I heard the quiet of his eyes.
I heard the candle flame stand still.
I saw the long line of her jaw become
Too beautiful to bear. I was a child.
I lifted my empty spoon and licked the light.

HOTEL CARLYLE, NEW YORK

Inside the dining room it was snowing.
Men and linen stayed warmly candlelit.
The gay waiters returned from the heat of the kitchen
Unsmilingly cold as Lenin.
Women were vast white estates
Measured in versts.
The chandeliers were Fabergé sleighs
Flying behind powerful invisible horses,
Powerful invisible forces,
On runners of serfs over
The foam of snowdrifts of fine linen.
Take us
Home from the ball
Through the dark, in the deepening snow!
Through an onion-domed metropolis,
Down the ghosts of avenues,
Furs covered us as we raced through the silence
Of the candlelight of the Carlyle.
Our corner table in the back room was
The last White Russian winter of the Czar
Across from a robed Black African
Ambassador to the UN and his entourage
At the height (in the depth) of the 1991 recession.
It was 1917.
I couldn't overthrow anything.
You were my height and depth.

We were a perfect fit.
You were my destiny if only
I would overthrow myself and take over!
Your grave dignity looked at me until I saw
The long line of your jaw become
Too beautiful to bear.
Life achingly said, *Do* something!
And I didn't dare.

DAS KAPITAL

The without blinds or curtains and incapable of being opened
That let the light in after dawn to mop the blood up into day
Are lighted up tonight because people are working late.
Some of the office towers are lighted up empty
So they can be cleaned overnight,
Hours the undertaker needs
To prepare the corpse to last.
The Gross Anatomy class debris
Becomes the Puerto Rican Day parade.
And the clean-up after becomes
Bare clean stainless steel tables with drains.

CHRISTMAS

A man comes in from the whirl
To a room where he does yoga
High above the homeless. He runs smack
Into still space.
He sits in the air.
He hangs upside down to the floor.

A forest of severed trees,
A million needles on sale,
Christ has fragrant breath.
He faints into heightened awareness.
He levitates to the Cross.
He comes to in his own arms.

MOOD INDIGO

One was blacker.
The other one was frightened.
They cut the phone wires.
They used my neckties.
They had me on my stomach.
They tied a hangman's noose around my neck
And stretched the rope of neckties down my back
To my wrists and ankles.
The slightest movement choked me.
He grabbed a carving knife I had
And stabbed me in the temple over and over,
While his partner looked on in horror,
And never even broke the skin,
A technique used in Vietnam.
He find the biggest knife he can
An stab this white boy pretty good
An never even break the skin,
A torture used in Vietnam.
A war there is
And stuck it in a sideburn hard
And didn't even scratch the surface.

NOON

A shallow, brutal flood of energy
With high cheekbones and almond eyes.
Cow-eyed bull with a vagina seeing red everywhere.
The *muleta* in the mirror between her thighs.
She sits down naked in front of herself.
Arouses her. Her fury
Flattens Holland and then floods it.

The shallow, brutal flood of energy
Has the bones and Hera's eyes.
The cow-eyed bull with a vagina seeing red everywhere
On fire in a room of Rubenses.
A little girl in the Rubens Room
Is feminism, sword in hand.
The *muleta* trembles in the mirrored hand teasingly. *¡Toro!*

Her fantasy is to have said to a god deeply
Asleep beside her in bed, in a normal voice, "How did you
    sleep?"
Waking the bastard up. *¡Olé!*
7:00. The sun is in heaven.
9:00. The blue is nude.
Noon. The Sag Harbor noon
Siren goes off. The garden flows

Back and forth. There's a breeze
To help with and fan the gross.

The mirrored suit of lights goes rigid
Shaking the trembling *muleta*. The raw sword asks the
    hairy hump,
The battered, beaten, victimized and sweetened,
Wounded, weakened, tenderized, and moaning to die, to
    charge. The stadium
Of right-thinking women roars. Bleeds, bellows and roars.

Vive l'amour! Vive la mort!

SPRING

I want to date-rape life. I kiss the cactus spines.
Running a fever in the cold keeps me alive.
My twin, the garbage truck seducing Key Food, whines
And dines and crushes, just like me, and wants to drive.
I want to drive into a drive-in bank and kiss
And kill you, life. Sag Harbor, I'm your lover. I'm
Yours, Sagaponack, too. This shark of bliss
I input generates a desert slick as slime.

DUNE ROAD, SOUTHAMPTON

The murderer has been injecting her remorselessly
With succinylcholine, which he mixes in her daily insulin.
She's too weak to give herself her shots. By the time she has
     figured it out,
She is helpless.

She can't move any part of her face.
She can't write a note.
She can't speak
To say she hasn't had a stroke.

It's terrifying that she's aware
That something terrible is being done to her.
One day he ups the dose. And gets scared.
She has to be rushed to the local hospital and intubated.

They know at the hospital who she is,
One of the richest women in the world.
The murderer hands the attending a faked M.R.I.
It flaunts the name of a world authority. Showing she has
     had a stroke.

The neurologist on call introduces herself to the murderer
     and concurs.
Locked-in Syndrome, just about the worst.
Alive, with staring eyes.
The mind is unaffected.

And with the patient looking on expressionlessly,
Screaming don't let him take me home, without a sign or
    sound,
The doctor tells the murderer he can take her home,
If that's their wish.

Their little beach house has forty rooms.
Her elevator is carved mahogany.
The Great Gatsby swimming pool upstairs is kept full and
    never used.
Her tower bedroom flies out over the winter ocean, spreading
    its wings.

Mother, you're going to die,
He tells her, once they're alone.
You have the right to remain silent.
I'm making a joke.

I'll read you your rights.
He takes a syringe.
A woman has the right to bare arms. I particularly like
    them bare.
I might as well be talking to cement.

LONDON

IN MEMORIAM

Great-grandson of George Boole as in Boolean algebra.
First in his class at Cambridge till he received an inheritance.
Spent it all brilliantly in a flash flood of champagne.
Loved girls and genius. Loved Lord Rothschild his friend.

After a gentleman's Third fled to Paris.
Out of money but life was sweet.
Whisky and style and car-running across borders.
Imprisoned in Spain terrifying.

Meanwhile his father with whom he'd almost had a
    rapprochement died.
Rothschild visited him in prison once.
How can a boy renounce himself? He began.
But years later he was wonderfully still the same.

Letting rooms to pretty lodgers.
Selling off the Georgian silver piece by piece.
Fired as the engineering consultant for refusing to lie to
    England.
British Steel tried hard to ruin him but he won.

Stuttered and lisped and wouldn't look you in the eye
In a lofty gwandly Edwardian way.
Jimmy, in America it'll make you seem shifty.
Laughter and delight and he looks you in the eye for a second.

THE GREAT DEPRESSION

Noël Coward sweeps into a party late in 1928
In evening clothes, London.
Spotting the other divinity
In the room, twenty-year-old Tallulah Bankhead standing
    on her head,
Her dress down over her head,
No underpants, no face,
Too lovely, her whole life ahead of her—
Time for a Coward mot.
Hair slick, svelte in black and white, in tails,
Coward sublimely drawls,
Ah, Tallulah—
Always standing there with her mouth hanging open.

PARIS & TAHITI

THE BALLAD OF LA PALETTE

I fly to Paris with the English language
To write a script set in Tahiti.

This will be translated into French for the cast
By a son of the Hollywood blacklist.

The wife of the Hollywood blacklist son has cancer,
Only it will turn out she doesn't.

The Cajun singer on a CD
The movie director plays for me

We meet with an hour later
Outside in the light at La Palette.

We discuss a score,
A young Rimbaud good ole boy.

His week of concerts has sold out.
He brings the bayou to the Seine.

The overloaded sound system howls.
Testing, un, deux, trois.

With kids, has cancer,
Only doesn't.

Down in the bayou,
They hunt in the middle of the night with flashlights.

The spotted Catahoula hound, pink as a pig,
With the strangest voice you ever heard,

Trees the trembling prey
Without a word.

ANYONE WITH THE WISH

The lagoon of the biggest atoll in the world,
So wide across you can't see the other shore,
Is soft as dew.
Water is love
In Rangiroa.

Fish move away from you without fear,
Like buffalo on the plains before they disappeared.
The boat far above you on the surface waits,
The pale hull,
The motor as gonads.

You haven't come here only for the shark show.
Their fixed smiles glide.
Their blank eyes go along for the ride.
They bury their face in life explosively,
And shake their head back and forth to tear some off.

Every day a guide sets out a bait
So anyone with the wish can swim with the sharks,
And circle the meat,
And feel close to the teeth.
Sharks swim in the love.

THE RESUMPTION OF NUCLEAR TESTING
IN THE SOUTH PACIFIC

People in their love affairs.
People in their loneliness.

People in their beds alone.
People in each other's arms.

I woke up this morning.
I went to sleep last night.

I woke up this morning.
I went to sleep last night.

The beauty of Tahiti.
That lagoon in Huahiné.

Manta rays were mating.
One on top the other.

Venus, with Chinese eyes,
On the motu at Maupiti.

I wish I was a head of state.
I'd wave away my bodyguards.

I'd never been unhappy.
Now, I would never be.

A *force de frappe* is Gaston
    Flosse.
Tahitians always call him
    Gaston.

Gaston did this. Gaston said
    that.
Nobody better mess with
    Gaston!

The president of French
    Polynesia,
Gaston Flosse, has flown in to
    Paris.

Their Kingfish, their Huey
    Long,
Is very close to Jacques Chirac.

They're strolling down the rue
    de Seine.
Chirac is France's president.

FASTER

A GALLOP TO FAREWELL

Three unrelated establishments named Caraceni in Milan
On streets not far apart make custom suits for men.
They are the best,
Autistically isolated in the pure,
Some might say in the pure
Pursuit of gracefully clothing manure.
Superb, discreet, threading their way to God,
The suits curve with beauty and precision,
Perfection on the order of Huntsman in Savile Row
And their jacket cutter, Mr. Hall.

The attitude to take to shoes is there is Lobb.
The one in Paris, not the one in London.
No one has surpassed
The late George Cleverley's lasts,
The angle in of the heel, the slightly squared-off toe, the line,
Though Suire at Lobb is getting there.
His shoes fit like Paradise by the third pair.
Like they were Eve. The well-dressed man,
The vein of gold that seems inexhaustible,
Is a sunstream of urine on its way to the toilet bowl.

A rich American sadist had handcuffs made at Hermès
To torture with beauty the Duchesse d'Uzès.
A cow looking at the understated elegance would know
Simplicity as calm as this was art.

A briefcase from Hermès
Is ravishing and stark.
Flawless leather luxury made for horses out of cows
Is what the horsy cows grazing daily in the Faubourg
    St-Honoré store
Want to buy. Tour group cows in a feeding frenzy
Devour everything like locusts.

There are travelers who prefer the British Concorde to the
    French
For the interior in beige and gray.
Hermès has created a carry-on in water buffalo
For them called the Gallop.
Their seat is in the first cabin.
Three kinds of Caraceni suits chose the aisle.
The most underrated pleasure in the world is the takeoff
Of the Concorde and putting off the crash
Of the world's most beautiful old supersonic plane, with no
    survivors,
In an explosion of champagne.

A VAMPIRE IN THE AGE OF AIDS

He moves carefully away from the extremely small pieces
Of human beings spread around for miles, still in his leather seat.
He looks like a hunchback walking in the Concorde chair,
Bent over, strapped in, eyes on the ground
To avoid stepping on the soft.
He will use his influence to get
The cockpit voice recorder when it is recovered copied.
He loves the pilot in the last ninety seconds'
Matter-of-factness turning into weeping screams,
Undead in the double-breasted red velvet smoking jacket
    Huntsman made.

ANOTHER MUSE

Another muse appeared, but dressed in black,
Which turned to skin the minute the light was out.
He had become a front without a back.
Arousal was a desert with a spout.

A string of women like a string of fish
Kept dangling in the water to keep them alive.
Washed down with Lynch-Bages to assuage the anguish
Of eating red meat during a muff dive.

One woman, then another, then another.
Drops of dew dropped into a flat green ocean.
They leaked purity and freshness, and mother.
The glass eye of each dewdrop magnified his lack of emotion.

You get a visa and some shots and buy
Provisions for the Amazon and fly
Instead to Africa and tell them I
Will always be your friend and then you try.

He was too busy musing to unchain them,
The women on a string inside the slave pen.
Feminists in nylons in his brain stem.
Escaped slaves recaptured. They crave men.

Women with shaved legs. Women in bondage.
Come out of the closet in their leg irons.
Hooded and gagged and garter-belted Lynch-Bages.
He hears the distant screaming of the sirens.

He lifts his glass. He bows. Testosterone,
The aviation fuel that gives him wings,
Drinks to the gods. His kamikaze starts its flight from his zone
For her zone. Redlined, on full honk, he sings.

RED GUARDS OF LOVE

The Red Guards of love rhythmically stomp their feet
In the stands as their leaders denounce themselves and beg
    to be retrained.
Venus is dancing a tango called *Banco!* (as in baccarat).
She's wearing donkey's ears. She's wearing an amazing necklace
Of fetus heads.
The Guards rove through the modern cities,
Stoning to death the busts they don't like in the libraries.
The hypnotic suit of rights very slowly struts.

YANKEE DOODLE

Hart Crane wrote *The Bridge*—
The Great American Hart Attack stampedes
Rush hour to a standstill in every stanza.
The John Philip Souza outburst of trombones,
And fireworks powdering the summer night,
Are very American Charles Ives. Nowadays,
When an earring in one ear makes a pioneer,
Gender Studies find *Tender Buttons*
Is all about the sacred body
Of the rhino and author, Miss Stein,
And parts of her companion, Miss Toklas.
Leonard Bernstein pounces on the piano
To illustrate the point literally with his dick.
Now, Robert Frost is different.
Someone saw Frost
Whipping a tree. I would like to strip
You and whip you till I see Stars and Bars,
O big American Beauty.

OVID, *METAMORPHOSES* X, 298–518

A daughter loved her father so much
She accused him of sexual abuse.
But I am getting ahead of my story.
Ten years after
He had simply been being a good father
She made the charge.
But I am ruining it.
Not that the man was ever told.
And when the accused is not even advised
He has been accused,
And is therefore deprived of a chance to defend himself,
    society—
Shit! the teleprompter stopped—
Which camera is on?
So it goes these days
With the help of radical feminist therapy
Redressing so many obvious wrongs.
Also because the specialists
Advise against confronting the incestuous rapist
Who may of course have done nothing and be innocent,
But who if he has will deny it to the grave.
One slightly feels he must have done something for the charge
In the first place to have been made.

Muse, put your breast in my mouth
If you want me to sing.
(Fuck the muse.)

Sunlight yellow as a canary.
Perfume from the garden made the room tropical.
The maid in her uniform struggles to draw the heavy curtains.
Darkness in spasms spreads as she tugs.

Light covers the hot and humid girl on the bed
And then is yanked away
By the maid. The last light the maid sees slants across
The girl's eyes and nose like a blindfold.
One of the eyes is green as an emerald.
The fourteen-year-old nose is classical.
The eyes are open in the darkness.
Darkness shrink-wraps her
And where her hands are.
The maid leaves the room adjusting herself.

Please,
The girl says to her father, Please
Let me go to Harvard, Daddy.
They are on a cruise.
The water the white ship cuts through is flowers.
The tube they lean their elbows on is warm.
The sky is black. The stars are out.
White birds fly overhead in the middle of the ocean.
Bam bam
Men are shooting skeet on a higher deck.
Her mother is up there shooting.
The girl is in the stateroom with her father
Who is panting as if he were
Having a heart attack while she undresses.
She can't stop herself.
They are doing it.

The maid comes in the room without knocking.
It is time to wake the princess from her nap.
She pulls the curtains back
And finds the girl
Standing naked on a chair.

She has a noose around
Her neck attached to nothing,
Which is a metaphor for love.

If you really love your father that much,
The maid says an hour later
To the naked girl in her arms,
I will have to do something.

It happens that
The girl's mother is off at Canyon Ranch,
Best of the Fat Farms, getting in shape.
She has been there already a week,
And the king is extremely interested when he is told
One of the women in the palace
Is obsessed with His Highness.
Oh, really, how old?
Oh, young, about your daughter's age.

The girl walks into her dream
Late that night when the maid arrives to take her
To her father.
A bird throbbily coos in the warm darkness outside.
The night air smells so sweet.

She immediately trips and knows perfectly well
What that means, but can't, won't, not.
The maid is sexually excited.
The virgin is in a delirium.

It's the familiar fear-of-heights terror
Of being irresistibly drawn
To the edge. You fall
From the other side of the edge toward the street
To get to Mars.
She feels the moisture of desire.

The man is fast asleep after a lot of drinking
So when the maid says, This is the one,
In the dark room he at first grabs the maid
Who redirects his hands and he is immediately
Inside the girl.

For the next two nights the maid
Stands outside in the corridor perspiring,
With her eyes tightly shut, clenching and unclenching her fists.

The father has hidden a flashlight next to his penis in the
        darkness
In the bed so he can see
Who it is the next night,
When it dawns on him he can simply turn the light on.
He does and tries to kill her,
But she is too fast.
The next thing he hears she is in Sagaponack.

She backtracks to Islip and flies
Out West and keeps going to Hawaii and Bali and on.
She sees the Komodo dragons twenty feet long
And carnivorous and fast and keeps going.
Sri Lanka, southern India, Myanmar
(Where Ne Win, the senile military dictator who has tried
        to ruin
Rangoon and everywhere else and everyone, still keeps
        the daughter
Of the great patriot democrat of the country
Under house arrest, but one day that will end).
For nine months she travels, pregnant.

On the day she turns into a tree,
She gives birth to a boy.

HEART ART

A man is masturbating his heart out,
Swinging in the hammock of the Internet.
He rocks back and forth, his cursor points
And selects. He swings between repetitive extremes
Among the come-ons in the chat rooms.
But finally he clicks on one
World Wide Web woman who cares.

Each of her virtual hairs
Brings him to his knees.
Each of her breasts
Projects like a sneeze.
He hears her dawning toward him as he reads her dimensions,
Waves sailing the seas of cyberspace—
Information, zeros-and-ones, whitecaps of.

Caught in a tangle of Internet,
Swinging in the mesh to sleep,
Rocking himself awake, sailing the virtual seas,
A man travels through space to someone inside
An active matrix screen. Snow falls.
A field of wildflowers blooms. Night falls.
Day resumes.

This is the story about humans taking over
The country. New York is outside

His study while he works. Paris is outside.
Outside the window is Bologna.
He logs on. He gets up.
He sits down. A car alarm goes off
Yoi yoi yoi yoi and yips as it suddenly stops.

Man has the takeover impact
Of an asteroid—throwing up debris, blotting out the sun—
Causing the sudden mass extinction
Of the small bookstore
At the millennium. The blood from the blast cakes
And forms the planet's new crust:
A hacker in Kinshasa getting it on with one in Nome.

Their poems start
With the part about masturbating the heart—
Saber cuts whacking a heart into tartare—
Heart art worldwide,
Meaning that even in the Far East the subject is love.
Here in the eastern United States,
A man is masturbating his art out.

An Ice Age that acts hot
Only because of the greenhouse effect
Is the sort of personality.
Beneath the dome of depleted ozone, they stay cold.
Mastodons are mating on the Internet
Over the bones of dinosaur nuclear arms,
Mating with their hands.

SPIN

A dog named Spinach died today.
In her arms he died away.
Injected with what killed him.
Love is a cup that spilled him.
Spilled all the Spin that filled him.
Sunlight sealed and sent.
Received and spent.
Smiled and went.

PUBERTY

I see a first baseman's mitt identical to mine
On the right hand of the best who ever lived.

The dark deep claw of leather
Called a trapper hungrily flaps shut and open

While Stan Musial stands there glowing and magnified
In Sportsman's Park on the red dirt behind the bag,

A crab whose right claw is huge,
Costumed legs apart and knees slightly bent,

Springy on spikes, a grown man on springs,
Source of light with wings

(And when he is at bat, one of the beautiful swings).
The pitcher goes into the windup and rears back with desire.

Stan the Man pounds our glove
Broken in with neat's-foot oil.

We get a runner caught in a rundown between first and
    second.
I can't get the ball back out of the pocket

To throw to the pitcher covering second in time.
Then fifty years pass.

Nothing is next.

THE INFINITE

The beauty of the boy had twisted
Into a shape brain damage has.
Into the room walked a twenty-year-old
Helix with a head
Lopsidedly.

The radiant
Grimness of the Shostakovich
Fifteenth Quartet, the last,
Most austere, most beautiful solemn terror,
The most music one repeated note can make, put out green
        leaves.

The twentieth century was drawing
To a close with a foal caught in amber smiling
At his mother.
Whose infinite eyes as he limped
In the room smiled.

TRUE STORY

A gerbil running on an exercise wheel whirs away the hours
To eternity by reciting the *Iliad*.
Just a gentle gerbil under Joseph Stalin, the eagle Osip
    Mandelstam.
Biting the arctic stars, black sky,
Spruce trees line his lower jaw.
Stalin flutters like a moth against his hot light.
Lightning flutters against the hot night.

St. Petersburg and Moscow are having sexual intercourse
In a slaughterhouse,
And will produce many sons.
But in the meantime there are the mixed moans.
The cockroach telephones Boris Pasternak from the Kremlin
    to croon
His fellow poet will be all right—but adds, "You don't
    really say
Much to save your friend," and hangs up.

HOT NIGHT, LIGHTNING

The United Nations is listening
Via simultaneous translation to the poet Mandelstam.
Tier after tier of the Tower of Babel tribunal being
Breast-fed by their headsets hear his starry eyes,
Marbles of melody and terror.
PowerBooks, powder of the rhinoceros horn, delegates
In every kind of suit and sari and sarong and dream
Men and women around the round world wear, rip
The ribbon from a box of chocolates
And find inside his wife and him,
And hear him begging Nadezhda not to leave the box.
A United Nations of all the languages is going
Through the air, a motorcycle going fast
Into the Nevada desert,
The joy of the original
Into a beautiful emptiness.
Through the double-parked side streets of New York
Into a tunnel, under a river,
The joy of the original goes
Into a tile hole
Which amplifies the sound.

The leading edge of the wing is your face
That comes to earth to me.
I watch you wait.

A twentieth-century
Power outage brings the darkness back
In the vicinity of Jesus Christ, a Caucasian male.
I want the General Assembly to know
How China greets the day.
They don't like blonds and they don't like blacks.
The smell won't go away.
The smell of sperm on the edge of the axe.
Among them Mandelstam, among the millions.
Into the aurora borealis cathedral he walks, filling the choir.
He and the other children weave
A rose window with the face of Shakespeare as the rose.
The tale he tells is made of Northern Lights.
Hairs of titanium are the bridge cables, of spun glass.
Horror has been hammered
Into white gold and gold gold,
Benumbed. Stalin has become sweet butter and salt
On an ear of summer butter-and-sugar corn.
The phonograph record pinned
Under the needle reaches the scratch.
Don't stop *thump* don't stop *thump* don't stop.

Snow is falling.
A candle burns.
I watch you waiting for me to wake.

THE STORM

The perfect body of the yoga teacher
Stains a timeless pose.
Her perfect tan
Is an untouchable.

The beauty of her body
Is a storm
About to hit.
The monsoon air is rank and sweet.

Lightning storms a room
Which thunder overpowers
With stun grenades
That blind and deafen.

Her skin contains the storm
Inside the pose.
Rain squalls wash
The sidewalks raw.

The bombing run unleashes
Mushrooms on a path.
The Stealth flies unseen
Inside out.

High above the homeless,
Back and forth,
Job walks inside out
Weeping storms.

The widow throws her body
On her husband's pyre.
The pose is pain
About to fall in floods.

The goal is grain
Enough to feed the world.
Bodies floating down the Ganges
Do the pose but while they do

The king is entering the field.
The queen is entering a grove.
The king is singing to the troops.
The storm is starting.

LITTLE SONG

My tiny Pitts
Fifteen and a half feet long
Brightly painted so it can be seen easily
By the aerobatics judges on the ground
Is a star.

The invisible biplane
Parked on display in my living room
With an inferior roll rate cheerily
Outperforms the more powerful Sukhoi's
Loops and spins.

G's of the imagination fasten
My five-point harness
To the star upside down
The sky is my living room
A chuck behind each wheel.

EISENHOWER YEARS

Suddenly I had to eat
A slowly writhing worm
A woman warmed on a flat stone in a jungle clearing
Or starve. I had to charm a Nazi waving a Lüger
Who could help me escape from a jungle river port town or die.

I had to survive not being allowed to sit down,
For ten hours, in a Mexico City
Jail, accused of manslaughter because
My cab driver in the early-morning rush hour
Had killed a pedestrian and jumped out and run.

The prostitute even younger than I was that
I had spent the night with had been
So shy I had gone home with her to meet her parents
When she asked. In the Waikiki Club
Where she worked, I'd faced her machete-faced pimp wielding
        a knife.

At the Mayan Temple of the Moon, "that" instead of "whom,"
Which the explorer Richard Halliburton
Has written everyone must climb on a night of the full moon
At midnight who wants to say he or she has lived,
The guard dog woke the guard up.

I heard the lyrical barking from the top.
I saw the wink of the rifle barrel far below in the moonlight
    and hit
The deck like a commando on the ramp along the outside
    of the pyramid to hide.
When at last I looked up Orson Welles stood there, doe-eyed
    sombrero silence
Expecting a bribe. I walked with him all innocence down
    the ramp.

I walked past him out the gate and he fired.
I felt invulnerable, without feelings, without pores.
A week after I got back home to St. Louis I fainted
At the wheel of a car just after I had dropped off a friend,
And for four months in the hospital with a tropical disease I
    nearly died.

Suddenly in the jungle there was an American professor
    named Bud Bivins
Who had fled from Texas to avoid the coming nuclear war.
The Nazi found passage for us both on a tramp steamer
    which ran
Into a violent storm in the Gulf not long after Bivins had
    gone mad
And taken to pacing the deck all night after the cook had
    demanded

On the captain's behalf that we pay him more, on top of what
We'd already paid, or swim, with his butcher knife pointing
    to a thin line
Of green at the horizon, the distant jungle shore.
The captain would be delighted to let us off immediately if
    we wished.
No one saw Bivins when we reached port.

In the middle of the night a huge wave hit
The rotten boatload of tarantulas and bananas, slam-dunking
    us under.
The cook and all the others, including our captain,
Kneeled at the rail holding on, loudly praying, so who was
    at the wheel?
Bivins was last spied on the deck. I was sixteen.

VICTORY

Nothing is pure at 36,000 feet either.
Even in First, there is only more.
The wing is streaked
By the jet engine's exhaust. Sometimes
I stand outside a toilet
Which is occupied, staring out
A window somewhere over Malaysia at dawn.
I am the wing,
The thing that should be lift,
Soiled by power.

Make no mistake about the heat.
It also has to eat.
It eats the fuel it's fed.
It eats the air.
It eats the hair.
It eats what's there.
The jungle devours me with its eyes which are
Screamed skyscrapers of plasm.
I said dismal. I meant passion.
The sky unfreezes me alive.

There is heaven the mainland. And there is heaven the island.
There is the warm water of heaven between.
The Minister of Defense bull's-eyes on the helicopter pad
With security all around wearing a curly wire into one ear.

Code-named Big Fish, he likes Eau Sauvage
To be there ahead of him wherever he goes.
There is heaven the novel, and heaven the movie.
Below you is the sky at 35,000 feet.
Above you is the muezzin until it ends.
I have the lift, but think I ought to land.

The blank eye of the sky muezzins the faithless to rise
And face the heat
And urinate and defecate and eat and act
Another day.
I wish I knew your name.
Powerful forces have built a road
Through the jungle. Muslim apparently
Women fully clothed are apparently allowed to expose in the lucky
Warm water with their brown kids sporting like putti flying fish.
Quiet on the set, please, thank you. The actors are rehearsing.

My penis is full of blood for you
Probably won't win her hand.
But you bet
Susanna the movie has to pull in the Elders.
She has designs.
She was designed to. She is audience response questionnaire-
    designed to
Get them to feast their eyes.
They're sitting in the dark and certainly
They're in the dark about
The lights will go on and the vile will be caught by a
    questionnaire.

Jungle covers an island in the South China Sea.
The interior is the first step in.
Perpetual summer sleeps with sixteen kinds of snakes.
My penis is full of love for you starred
In a road movie with Dorothy Lamour and
The beautiful bay
Used to be a breeding ground for sharks
Where we're swimming now. The head
Of the British fleet, here for the joint
Naval exercises, told me he remembered it well, charming man.

The Steadicam glides everywhere,
Holding its head in the air like a King Cobra.
The ecology
Of the island is fragile, but the second airport will never be
    built.
This isn't Acapulco 1949 about to Big Bang.
You step into the jungle and it's thick.
You step into the warm water and it's thin.
But nothing jiggles the Steadicam.
The poisonous viper is authorized to use deadly force
Only on the jungle path to the waterfall above the golf
    course.

Someone has seen a ten-foot lizard
Near the set. Someone was seen feeding a monkey
Bananas. The set itself is a subset of itself,
A jungle set in the jungle.
Islam is aerosolized into the atmosphere,
Coating the jungle scenes with time.

St. Agatha is the martyr whose breasts got hacked off,
But in the movie they don't.
The breasts that don't get removed
Anticipate the replenishing monsoon.

God is everywhere you're not,
And you are everywhere. I wish I knew your name.
Congestion in the brain is cleared
By the tropical haze which mists the coconut palms
And by the horrible heat of heaven. Oddly sudden
Mountains rise right out of the sea, jungle-clad. Hairy
Angels are friendly, but not too friendly.
Palm trees can mean Palm Beach,
But where the monkeys are semi-tame
We are semi-saved.

I never sleep on planes, but woke
Belted in, seat upright, table stowed,
To the roar of the reverse thrust,
Semi-saved. I undressed into the ocean
Surrounded by security and businessmen talking into
        cellular phones.
The jungle is within. The jungle also comes down
To the heavenly warm water lapping the sand.
The jungle is the start and the jungle is the end.
The jungle is behind. The jungle is ahead.
Ahead of me is heaven.

VERMONT

The attitude of green to blue is love.
And so the day just floats itself away.
The stench of green, the drench of green, above
The ripples of sweet swimming in a bay
Of just-mowed green, intoxicates the house.
The meadow goddess squeaking like a mouse
Is stoned, inhales the grass, adores the sky.
The nostrils feed the gods until the eye
Can almost see the perfume pour the blue.
A Botticelli ladled from a well,
Your life is anything you want it to—
And loves you more than it can show or tell.

MILAN

RACINE

When civilization was European,
I knew every beautiful woman
In the Grand Hôtel et de Milan,
Which the Milanese called "The Millin,"
Where Verdi died, two blocks from La Scala,
And lived in every one of them
Twenty-some years ago while a motorcycle was being made
For me by the MV Agusta
Racing Department in Cascina Costa,
The best mechanics in the world
Moonlighting for me after racing hours.
One of the "Millin" women raced cars, a raving beauty.
She owned two Morandis, had met Montale.
She recited verses from the Koran
Over champagne in the salon and was only eighteen
And was too good to be true.
She smilingly recited Leopardi in Hebrew.
The most elegant thing in life is an Italian Jew.
The most astonishing thing in life to be is an Italian Jew.
It helps if you can be from Milan, too.
She knew every *tirade* in Racine
And was only eighteen.
They thought she was making a scene
When she started declaiming Racine.
Thunderbolts in the bar.
With the burning smell of Auschwitz in my ear.

With the gas hissing from the ceiling.
Racine raved on racing tires at the limit of adhesion.
With the gas hissing from the showers.
I remember the glamorous etching on the postcard
The hotel continued to reprint from the original 1942 plate.
The fantasy hotel and street
Had the haughty perfect ease of haute couture,
Chanel in stone. A tiny tailored doorman
Stood as in an architectural drawing in front of the façade and
    streamlined
Cars passed by.
The cars looked as if they had their headlights on in the rain,
In the suave, grave
Milanese sunshine.

MILAN

This is Via Gesù.
Stone without a tree.
This is the good life.
Puritan elegance.
Severe but plentiful.
Big breasts in a business suit.
Between Via Monte Napoleone and Via della Spiga.

I draw
The bowstring of Cupid's bow,
Too powerful for anything but love to pull.

Oh the sudden green gardens glimpsed through gates and the
    stark
Deliciously expensive shops.
I let the pocket knives at Lorenzi,
Each a priceless jewel,
Gods of blades and hinges,
Make me late for a fitting at Caraceni.

Oh Milan, I feel myself being pulled back
To the past and released.
I hiss like an arrow
Through the air,
On my way from here to there.
I am a man I used to know.

I am the arrow and the bow.
I am a reincarnation, but
I give birth to the man
I grew out of.
I follow him down a street
Into a restaurant I don't remember
And sit and eat.

A Ducati 916 stabs through the blur.
Massimo Tamburini designed this miracle
Which ought to be in the Museum of Modern Art.

The Stradivarius
Of motorcycles lights up Via Borgospesso
As it flashes by, dumbfoundingly small.
Donatello by way of Brancusi, smoothed simplicity.
One hundred sixty-four miles an hour.
The Ducati 916 is a nightingale.
It sings to me more sweetly than Cole Porter.
Slender as a girl, aerodynamically clean.
Sudden as a shark.

The president of Cagiva Motorcycles,
Mr. Claudio Castiglioni, lifts off in his helicopter
From his ecologically sound factory by a lake.
Cagiva in Varese owns Ducati in Bologna,
Where he lands.
His instructions are Confucian:
Don't stint.

Combine a far-seeing industrialist.
With an Islamic fundamentalist.
With an Italian premier who doesn't take bribes.
With a pharmaceuticals CEO who loves to spread disease.
Put them on a 916.

And you get Fred Seidel.

BOLOGNA

A PRETTY GIRL

Umber, somber, brick Bologna.
They could use some Miami Jews
In this city of sensible shoes.

In the city of Morandi,
The painter of the silence
Of groups of empty bottles,
Arcades of demure
Men dressed in brown pneumonia
Look for women in the fog.

Bare, thick, spare, pure,
Umber, somber, brick Bologna.
This year's fashion color is manure,
According to the windows
Of fogged-in manikins
In Piazza Cavour.
Reeking of allure,
Arcades of demure
Young women dressed in odorless brown pneumonia
Give off clouds of smoke,
Dry ice in the fog.

Bare, thick, spare, pure:
Shaved heads reading books flick
Their cigarettes away and cover their mouths with their scarfs,

Leaned against the radical Medical School,
Punks with stethoscopes, horoscopes.
They listen to the heart with the heart,
Students in the medieval streets.

Their tangerine fingernails heal
The Emergency Room in gloves
Till dawn, and still come out eager to Day-Glo Bologna.
The tangerine tirelessly sheds disposable latex
Gloves until the day glows.
Emergency path lighting
On the airplane floor has led me to the exits
Through the cold and the fog.
Follow the tangerine path through the dark and the smoke.
Beneath the unisex jeans
Is cunnus soft as shatoosh.

The Communist mayor who underwrites the Morandi Museum
Takes a right-wing industrialist through the silence.

And the Ducati motorcycle factory
In Via Cavalieri Ducati breathes to life
Another piece of sculpture that goes fast.
Art and engineering meet and make
A brain wave
Of beauty suitable to ride.

The advice of my physician
Is turn sixty.

I limit lovemaking to one position,
Mounted on a Ducati, monoposto:
Equivalent to warm sand as white as snow,
And skin as brown as brandy,
And swimming in the blue of faraway.

A well-dressed man is lying on a bed
With Leopardi in his arms.
The fog outside the window is Bologna.
He does the dead man's float
Next to the sleek hull of the sloop *A Pretty Girl,*
Stuck in a sheet of glue
Which extends for a hundred miles
Without a sip of wind,
Under a sky.
The blue is infinite.
He can see three miles down.
He free-floats in glass in his body temperature.
He does not know yet that he has dived in
Forgetting to let the ladder down,
And he does not know
He cannot climb back up.
There are no handholds.
The sloping sides are smooth.
The deck too high.
She heads for the horizon under full sail
In his flash hallucination. You never
Leave no one on board,
But he does not know yet what has happened since
A Pretty Girl is not going anywhere.

The sailboat pond in Central Park
Is where a boy's days were a breeze.
He does the dead man's float
Next to the motionless boat,
But in art there is no hope.
Art is dope.

The fog glows,
Tangerine toward sundown.

The Communist mayor who is said
To be tough but fair
Is waiting.

Take me, silence.

GOING FAST

GOING FAST

I
Extra Heartbeats

Red
As a Ducati 916, I'm crazed, I speed,
I blaze, I bleed,
I sight-read
A Bach Invention.

I'm at the redline.
When I speak you hear
The exhaust note of a privateer.

I see an audience of applause.
Pairs of hands in rows.
Palestinian and Jew.
And black and brown and yellow and red.
Wedding rings wearing watches
Pound Life lines into foam.
Fate lines. Date lines. Date palms. Politics. Foam.

The air blurs with the clapping.
The sidewalks sizzle with mica.
The colors tremble and vibrate.
The colors in the garden start to shake apart
While the applause swells.

The four walls of the world pump,
Pump their chemicals.

When I give my lectures,
The tachometer reads at the redline.
When I speak you hear
The exhaust note of a privateer.

The flutter in my chest is extra heartbeats,
My ectopy.

And Rabin is calling Arafat.
And Arafat, Rabin.
The Touch-tone beeps are rising
To the sky like the bubbles in champagne.

The chemo is killing the white cells.
The white cells are killing the red cells.

They'll have to kill me first.

They'll find me
Flying on the floor.

II
Candle Made from Fat

The most beautiful motorcycle ever made
Was just made.
I ride to Syria
To Assad on one.

A hundred and sixty-four miles an hour
On the 916
Makes a sound,
My friend, makes a sound.

I seek the most beautiful terror.
Massimo Tamburini designed it.
I ride to Syria
To President Assad on one.

Hafez al-Assad, a hundred and sixty-four miles an hour
On the Ducati 916
Makes a sound,
My friend, makes a certain sound.

A group that calls itself
The Other Woman,
In southern Lebanon, apparently with money
From Iran, is assembling the bomb.

It's red,
Flying through the desert
Toward the border with Israel,
As I approach my sixtieth birthday.

The school bus entering the outskirts
Of Jerusalem is full.
The motorcycle
Is screaming, God is great.

The kangaroo effect
Is boing-boing-boing as the white light bounds away,
Leaving in their blood the burning curls
Of Jewish boys and girls.

III
Lauda, Jerusalem

My violent Honda 125cc Grand Prix racer
Is the size of a bee.
It is too small to ride
Except for the joy.

My on-fire 1996 RS125R
Flies on its little wings,
A psalmist, all stinger,
On racing slicks.

It absolutely can't stop
Lifting its voice to scream.
It mounts the victory podium.
Lauda, Jerusalem, Dominum.

I am a Jew.
I am Japan.
I shift gears over and over.
I scream to victory again and again.

Fall leaves inflame the woods.
It is brilliant to live.
The sorrow that is not sorrow,
The mist of everything is over everything.

IV
Poem Does

The god in the nitroglycerin
Is speedily absorbed under the tongue
Till it turns a green man red,
Which is what a poem does.
It explosively reanimates
By oxygenating the tribe.

No civilized state will execute
Someone who is ill
Till it makes the someone well
Enough to kill
In a civilized state,
As a poem does.

I run-and-bump the tiny
Honda 125cc Grand Prix racer. Only
Two steps and it screams. I
Slip the clutch to get the revs up, blipping and getting
Ready not to get deady,
Which also is what a poem does.

They dress them up in the retirement centers.
They dress them up in racing leathers.
They dress them up in war paint and feathers.
The autumn trees are in their gory glory.
The logs in the roaring fire keep passing
The peace pipe in pain, just what a poem does.

Stanza No. 5. We want to be alive.

Line 26. We pray for peace.

Line 27. The warrior and peacemaker Rabin is in heaven.

28. We don't accept his fate.

But we do. Life is going ahead as fast as it can,

Which is what a poem does.

V
Israel

An animal in the wild
Comes up to you in a clearing because it
Has rabies. It loves you. It does not know why.
It pulls out a gun.
You really will die.

The motorcycle you are riding
Is not in control of itself.
It is not up to you to.
The sky is not well.
It wants to make friends.

It stalks you to
Hold out its hand
At a hundred and sixty-four miles an hour.
It asks you to
Take down your pants.

Daphne fleeing Apollo
Into the Sinai shrinks to a bonsai.
The Jewish stars that top the crown
Prime Minister Rabin is wearing
As he ascends to heaven assassinated, twinkle.

The main tank holds the dolphins.
Land for peace is not for them.

Daphne fleeing Apollo
Across the desert of your desk becomes
In India a cow.

The icing on the cake
Is stone. The Ten Commandments
Are incised in it.
You take a bite
Of Israel and spit out teeth, señor.

You throw your head back and wheelie
On the RS125R
And the Ducati,
Surrounded by security rushing you forward,
Suddenly aware you have been shot.

VI
Killing Hitler

A Ducati Supermono walks down the aisle
At a hundred and forty-one miles an hour
To kiss the Torah, trumpeting,
An elephant downsized to a gazelle that devours lions.

Red Italian bodywork
Designed by the South African
Pierre Terblanche is sensuous lavish smoothness
With mustard-yellow highlights.

Even the instrument binnacle
Is beautiful and the green
Of the top triple clamp
Means magnesium, no expense spared, very trick.

The rabbi weighs only
301 lbs. with the tank full.
It wails straight
To the Wailing Wall.

It is big but being small
The Supermono has a mania.
The double con-rod balance system is elegance.
The total motorcycle bugles petite magnificence.

How to keep killing Hitler
Is the point.
How to be a work of art and win.
How to be Supermono and marry Lois Lane in the
   synagogue, and love.